Man's Inheritance

A Profile Of Mankind's
Spiritual & Material Acquisitions

By

Dr. Eddie Jernagin

Man's Inheritance

A Profile Of Mankind's
Spiritual & Material Acquisitions

By

Dr. Eddie Jernagin

Copyright @ 2014
All Rights Reserved
Printed in The United States of America

Published By:

ABM Publications
A division of Andrew Bills Ministries Inc.
PO Box 6811
Orange, CA 92863

www.abmpublications.com

ISBN: 978-1-931820-40-0

All scripture quotations, unless otherwise indicated are taken from the King James Version of the Bible, Public Domain. Those marked NIV are from the New International Version, copyright @ 1972, 1973, 1978, & 1984 by International Bible Society. Used by permission of Zondervan Publishing House. All rights reserved.

DEDICATION

This book is lovingly dedicated to my lovely wife,
Mamie Elizabeth Jernagin,
who has been my faithful companion
and my closest friend for many years.

TABLE OF CONTENTS

	Preface	7
	Introduction	11
1	Man's Origin And Fall	14
2	Evolution Vs. Creation	23
3	We Are Family	29
4	Singleness And Marriage	39
5	Abraham's Inheritance	45
6	God And The Israelites	55
7	Greed For Materialism	65
8	Determination	73
9	Inheriting Riches Through Thanksgiving And Praise	79
10	The Bible (God's Word)	87
11	Inheritance Of Love	97
12	The Supreme Sacrifice	105

13	Born Again	111
14	Faith	119
15	Healing	125
16	Time – Your Heritage	131
17	Omega	139
	About The Author	151
	More Available Books	153
	Ministry Contact Information	155

PREFACE

It is basically true that we profit from the mistakes of others. Yet, sometimes I wonder why man falls into the same vice as his predecessors. The one basic conclusion that I have reached is that man's rebellion against recognizing the will of God in directing his daily life is too often ignored. Consequently, without yielding to the Supreme Wisdom of God to guide his daily living, man becomes a victim of his own lust, zeal, greed and pride, ultimately leading to failure in his vain efforts to succeed without the help of his Maker.

Just as a little child needs parental guidance and love to develop into a respectable adult, so mankind in general needs the help of God to see where he has no insight and conquer what he cannot obtain on his own initiative to survive and succeed in this present world, as well as the world to come.

Man is incapable of controlling himself and the multiple problems that surrounds him. Therefore, he must rely upon a Wisdom that supersedes that of his own, because all of man's wisdom is vanity. I once heard a minister preaching a most profound sermon. During the course of his oral discourse, he said, *"Man has conquered the challenge of going to the moon and has learned to fly in the air like a bird, but in spite of this and other achievements that have been accomplished through his wisdom, he has not learned how to get along with his fellow man."*

God in His relationship to man as the Supreme Father teaches man to respect himself, as well as other human beings. God in history has been and always will be, the ultimate stabilizing factor in the unbalanced world of selfish man. He alone is the only one who can stabilize man, because He is the Supreme mind behind man's creation; man is His product. Therefore, as an inventor is to his invention, so God is to His creation.

The following pages of this book is but a minute paraphrase of man's spiritual and physical acquisitions in history. It is the writer's profound belief that, that which man has inherited has been greatly influenced by his subjection or disobedience to his Creator.

Man's life and eternal destiny is fashioned by his personal mode of living. He stands as a free moral agent at liberty to choose the way of good or evil. And the basis for which this good or evil can be judged is by the Divine standards of a Supreme Master Plan of rules and regulations initiated by God.

God's insurmountable love for His creation is expressed to its fullest in the atoning sacrifice of His son Jesus Christ for the sins and rebellion of mankind. In the final analysis, man's eternal inheritance will be determined by his acceptance or rejection of the ultimate gift of God's love – Jesus!

I have attempted to approach this subject matter with a prayerful heart and humbled attitude, seeking not to induce my own prejudicial opinions, but, rather correlating the episode of life's broad spectrum of events with the records of Biblical history to the dispensational period of grace, and finally, the end of time.

All scriptural quotations are from the Authorized King James version. When I have borrowed material from other sources, it is so specified before or after each quotation.

INTRODUCTION

It was on a warm summer evening on August 12, 1970. Though I usually fly to most of my revival meetings, I chose rather to take a few hours bus ride from Los Angeles, California, to a small little farming community in Farmington, New Mexico.

As we left the city of the Angeles (Los Angeles) people were stirring busily attending to their evening's activities. Briskly our driver drove through the crowded city streets with an assuring expertise. At last we reached the freeways and they were clustered as usual with every driver headed towards diverse destinations.

Venturing farther away from the hustle and bustle of the gigantic metropolis, I looked over my shoulder and saw the newly built monstrous skyscrapers peering through the density of the smoldering smog that usually surrounds the bustling city.

I reclined in my seat for the journey ahead. A soothing feeling of much needed relaxation came upon me as we proceeded farther away from the city and into the uninhabited areas of the vast golden countryside of sunny California.

Rolling steadily along the galloping slopes and hills of the Grand Canyon state of Arizona, I suddenly became captivated by the peacefulness of the parched desert land with its cluster of scattered bushes and cactus, and it background of mountain peaks, each seemed to be competing for superior rule in their towering height.

As our journey across the desert land continued, inquisitive thoughts dazzled across my mind. I began to wonder, for what purpose were mountains created, and why the creation of a vast picturesque dry desert? Could it be that it was just some mere happenstance with no particular purpose? Or was there some underlying motive for the being of such things?

Several hours had now passed since leaving Los Angeles, and day began to lose it's battle with time as dusk proudly took its stand for a brief few moments of glory. Then, suddenly, like a majestic miracle, flashing steaks of fiery lighting dashed across the darkened blue desert skies, and the deep golden moon began to stand out as a glowing beacon light illuminating the darkened heavens. As I looked miles ahead of me I saw what seemed to be a furious storm stirring in the distance, as the bold-faced mountains began to fade in the swift approaching grasp of night.

As quick as a flash, the unspeakable beauty of what I had seen completely overwhelmed me. It was then I whispered a brief prayer, *"God I thank you for the vastness of your beautiful creation."*

The desert which usually seemed useless and barren to me, with no specific purpose for being, now became a living testimony and memorial of God's love of beauty. The mountains began to take on a purpose for their existence as being God's way of letting me and millions of other Homosapiens be the fortunate recipients of the radiant beauty of His incomparable creation!

DR. EDDIE JERNAGIN

I believe in the brook as it wanders
from the hillside into glade;
I believe in the breeze as it whispers
When evening shadows fade.
I believe in the roar of the river,
as it dashes from high cascade;
I believe in the cry of the tempest
'mid the thunder's cannonade.
I believe in the light of shining stars,
I believe in the sun and the moon'
I believe in the flash of lighting,
I believe in the nigh bird's croon.
I believe in the faith of the flowers,
I believe in the rock and sod,
For in all of this appeareth clear
The handwork of God.

-Author Unknown

Chapter One

MAN'S ORIGIN AND FALL

Man was made in the image of God. He was made perfect in stature, free of guilt, void of sin and inheriting God-like characteristics from his Supreme Creator. In a secondary sense one might say that man was theoretically like a *"little god'* in his own right; in the sense that Almighty God who rules over heaven and earth gave him authority to have domination and rule:

> *"over the fish of the sea, and over the fowl of the air, and over the cattle, and over all the earth, and over every creeping thing that creepeth upon the earth."* (Genesis 1:26)

As a result of man's fall in the Garden of Eden those who became the offspring of Adam inherited the degraded sin nature which defiled Adam at the moment of his sinful gesture against the will of God.

Consequently, all humanity at the moment of conception now obtains a sinful nature, marring the image of God in man.

We read our daily newspaper, or watch a news bulletin on our television screens, or come in contact with any communication media, and are daily confronted with the distressing echoes of war, pestilence and violence. We commonly hear of raping of women and small girls; the murdering of innocent beings on our city streets in the darkness of night and the horror of a suicide. Often, we wonder why such damnable occurrences take place among the poor and ignorant, as well as the aristocratic and elite.

The answer to this prevailing question lies not within our intellectual philosophies or psychoanalysis, but rather in Holy Scriptures:

"Now the serpent was more subtle than any other beast of the field which the Lord God had made. And he said unto the woman, yea, hath God said, Ye shall not eat of every tree of the garden?

And the woman said unto the serpent, we may eat of the fruit of the trees of the garden: but of the fruit of the tree which is in the midst of the garden, God hath said, Ye shall not eat of it, neither shall ye touch it, lest you die.

And the serpent said unto the woman, ye shall not surely die: for God doeth know that in the day ye eat thereof, then your eyes shall be opened, and ye shall be as gods, knowing good and evil.

And when the woman saw that the tree was good for food, she took of the fruit thereof, and did eat, and gave unto her husband with her; and he did eat." (Genesis 3:1-6)

From the preceding scripture we see the channel through which the defilement of man's existence on earth came into being. Adam's disobedience led to his expulsion from a peaceful abode of utmost tranquility to a vast plan of sickness, disease, unrest and turmoil. It also led to a transformation of man's godly state of purity and innocence to what can be described as a *"filthy rag."*

"We are all as an unclean thing, and all our righteousness are as filthy rags and we all do fade as a leaf; and our iniquities, like the wind have taken us away." (Isaiah 64:6)

How wonderful and exciting it must have been for Adam to walk in the serenity of God, having no consciousness of hopelessness, sickness and disease; or the malignancy of sin feasting on the body, mind and soul of his being. Even the most ferocious beasts of the lower animal kingdom walked in the harmony and peace of God!

The state of every living creature, however, was adversely affected as a consequence of Adam's disobedience. The beasts of the field became antagonistic to the prevailing peace, harmony and love that once was a reality. Humanity was thrust into a state of cataclysmic confusion and total disharmony with God. The very ground that man walked upon became cursed, yielding forth thorns and thistles. Originally man was made to live forever, but now the blackness of death became his destined plight. God said,

"In the sweat of thy face shalt thou eat bread, till thou return unto the ground; for out of it wast thou taken; for dust thou art, and unto dust shalt thou return." (Genesis 3:19)

Since that dreadful day in the garden of Eden all posterity now inherits the sorrows of life.

The radiant splendor of twinkling stars; the rustling flow of rivers of crystal waters, the towering green trees in the forest; the mild autumn rains; even the soft summer breezes, were all created by Jehovah God for man's pleasure on planet earth. When God created man, He knew that the scenic display of "mother nature's wonders" would enhance the joy of living for all human beings and creatures living upon the gorgeous planet Earth!

Starvation and poverty were not in the Divine Plan of God for His created beings. It was not in the tender heart of Man's Founder to see men deprived of the necessities of life. Nevertheless, when the first woman (Eve) through pride yielded to the urging of the serpent rather than the will of God, satanic characteristics such as poverty, disease, starvation, etc., multiplied into what seems to be a prevailing curse in the life of fallen man.

Opposing Natures

Prior to man's fall in the Garden of Eden, he had no fusion of conflict within his soul of warring with two natures, he lived in harmony with God, having a depth of inner unopposed calmness. His nature was to do that which was in obedience to God, and he saw no evil or shame in the whole scheme of things created. Due to Adam's failure to uphold the command of God, it marked the beginning for the conflict of Adamic nature warring against the Supreme Spirit. Unfortunately, all men now have inherited an innate corruptible Adamic nature which wars against The Spirit of God and the image of God in man.

The Apostle Paul speaks of the strife between these two natures in his epistle to the Romans:

"For that which I do I allow not; for what I would, that do I not; but what I hate, that do I.

If then I do that which I would not, I consent unto the law that it is good. Now then it is no more I that do it, but sin that dwelleth in me. For I know that in me (that is in my flesh) dwelleth no good thing; for to will is present with me; and how to perform that which is good I find not. For the good that I would, I do not; but the evil which I would not, that I do.

Now if I do that I would not, it is no more I that do it, but sin that dwelleth in me." *(Romans 7: 15-20)*

In the preceding verses quite vivid is the personification of conflicting strife between these two natures.

The Adamic nature inherited by physical birth in sin, and the Divine Nature inherited by baptized believers through Grace into the body of Christ.

A detailed perspective of the new birth and divine nature will be expounded upon in greater detail in Chapter Thirteen.

Flame of the Spirit, and dust of the earth,
this is the making of man,
This is his problem of birth; born to all holiness,
born to all crime,
Heir of both worlds, on the long slope of time,
Climbing the path of God's plan; dust of the earth
in his error and fear,
Weakness and malice and lust; yet quivering up
from the dust,
Flame of the spirit, unleaping and clear, since
from God is its birth –
This is man's portion, to shape as he can, flame of
the spirit, and dust of the earth –
This is the making of man.

-Priscilla Leonard

Chapter Two

EVOLUTION VS CREATION

A variety of evolutionary theories regarding the origin of man were formulated during the latter part of the 19th Century. These theories consisted of basic factors considered to be supplements of Darwin's theory.

Charles Darwin (1790 -1882) is considered to be the most important figure in the history of organic evolutionary theory. As a youth he studied for the ministry, accepting the general concept of Biblical creation. It was during his voyage around the world between 1831-1836, that his concept of the origin of life began to change.

He became a devout student pursuing the study of organic evolution. Since then Darwin's theory of evolution as well as those of his predecessors, have been the subject of much controversy among scientists, clergymen and laity. In general it is the belief of evolutionists that mankind slowly evolved from lower forms of organic life in an evolutionary sequence from fish 155,000,000 years ago.

The amphibian (between the fish & reptiles) succeeded them 300,000,000 years ago. And were followed by reptiles approximately 250,000,000 years ago; and eventually by mammals 150,000,000 years ago. Approximately 19,000,000 years ago, according to scientists, the first likeness of man appeared in the ape family.

Actually, there is no real conflict between true science and God's creation. For all facts which science has discovered testify to the creative power and ability of the Spirit of Almighty God. One should become acutely aware, however, that theory is not science. Theory is void of conclusive facts; it is merely and assumption based upon human logic and speculations; it is a proposed explanation: Darwin's theory falls into this particular category. Science is based upon factual evidence. God's creation is *"fact"* because there is tangible evidence all around us. Man's existence is a fact. The Word of God which is indeed *"fact,"* states that:

"God created man in his own image."

(Genesis 1:27)

God being the great creator, and man being a recipient of his likeness also has the ability to create because of his intelligence inherited from God. Not from a fish or ape!

God has Supreme Intelligence and He sovereignly rules over the heavens and earth. Man has dominion over that which God has given him to subdue upon the earth. And by faith, the called of God's (Christian believers) accept the fact of God's Word that man was made from the "dust" of the earth by a miraculous act of God!

> *"And God made the beast of the earth after his kind, and cattle after their kind, and everything that creepeth upon the earth after his kind." (Genesis 1:25)*

Notice in the above passage of scripture that God made each beast of the earth after his kind. This simply means that the fish was made after the *"fish kind,"* the amphibian after the "amphibian kind" the ape after the *"ape kind"* and man in the image of "God Kind." Human kind is not a product of theoretical evolution, but a factual creation made in the image of a Supreme, intelligent God.

There is a broad gap between human intelligence and animal intelligence. Therefore, how can such superior intellect such as that of man evolve out of that which is lesser? And why, if man evolved from some lower source rather than the creative act of God, does he dominate the earth with such authority? Surely if man evolved from some lower being, that being should in fact be man's superior? This is a basic sequential trend of nature!

Scientists can dissect life to its finite degree, and in the final analysis, there must be a recognition of the creative omnipotence of God behind all human conception?

How poor, how rich, how abject, How august,
How complicate,
How wonderful is man! How passing wonder He
Who made him such?
Who centered in our make such strange extremes!
From different natures marvelously mixed,
Connection exquisite of distant worlds!
Distinguished link in being's endless chain,
Midway from nothing to the Deity!
A beam ethereal, sullied and absorb!
Though sullied and dishonored, still divine!
Dim miniature of greatness absolute! An heir of
glory! A frail child of dust!
Helpless immortal! Insect infinite! A worm!
A god! I tremble at myself,
And in myself am lost. At home a stranger,
Though wanders up and down,
Surprised, aghast, And wondering at her own.
How reason reels!

Oh! What a miracle is man! Triumphantly distressed!

What joy! What dread! Alternately transported and alarmed!

What can preserve my life! Or what destroy?

An angel's arm can't snatch me from the grave":

Legions of angels cannot confine me there!

-Edward Young

Chapter Three

WE ARE FAMILY

Imagine a world of total individual isolation! Needless to say, strong nations would be non-existent. The United States of America would be the *"Divided States of America."* The solidification of our armed forces as a cohesive united would make them ineffective to defend the nation! Human life would be as a *"divided house"* not able to stand!

When I was a student in high school I was a member of the concert choir. I remember vividly how we would sing a song with lyrics that expressed the following:

"*No man is an island; no man stands alone. Each man's joy is joy to me; each man's joy is my own. We need one another; so I will defend; each man as my brother, each man as my friend!"*

Inner Dependency

The preceding lyrics epitomizes a clear portrayal of inner dependency which is an integral part of life. God made it so. No matter how much we strive to be independent the fact still remains that the survival of humankind depends upon human coalition.

Creative Inventions

Think of all the technical, scientific, ingenious ideas, products and plans man has contributed to life for the convenience, survival and enjoyment of living. Jet aircraft, bullet trains, microwave ovens, laser beam technology, the automobile, etc.. Although the genius of these ideas may have come from the creative intellect of a unique elite; we all can benefit and enjoy these commodities on a massive scale!

No matter how a person might try to distance himself from others when all is said and done eventually they will have to depend in some measure upon others. This is an inherent fact of life.

Mutual Respect

We should daily strive to get along with each other in this world. Learning to respect the ethnicity as well as the diverse cultural uniqueness of our fellow man. This is why I personally advocate the integration of society. Integration provides an educational experience, and creates an atmosphere for an opportunity to exercise mutual respect. Harmony and inner personal relationships are vital to the strength of the human race. Without it, we weaken the fiber of our God given right of dominance we have been given to subdue the rest of creation. An examination of the triune oneness of the God Head (God the Father, Son, and Holy Spirit) reveals the fact of unequaled strength existing within the inseparable union of the Divine triune. Jesus said:

"I and My Father are one" *(John 10:30)* Therefore, we who are the offspring of our Creator should possess the same spirit of unity and harmony within the human family. How tragic it is indeed that within the human race

prejudice and discrimination degrades this unity among us!

If we believe in the Biblical account of creation, we cannot deny the fact that *"we are family."* This is an established fact that can not be altered by the antagonistic evils that are within the human family.

Although there are some exceptions, generally family ties are very special to most of us. There is a special bond which contributes to the strong adherence to family. This bond is influenced by blood ties and love and respect for our kin! This three fold bond when exercised toward your fellow man outside of the biological linage of immediate family demands a mutual reciprocation. Doing unto others as we desire others to do unto us; loving one's neighbor as one's own self is a noble experience. When this two way process is allowed to govern our actions towards our fellow man the strength of friendship grows stronger, contributing to the strength of human society. This mutual act also further enhances the testimony of our heritage as part of the family of God on earth!

The human family among all ideals, is of the highest order! When we fail to get along, allowing hatred and prejudice to divide our bond, we degrade the ideal of the family of God on earth, causing damnation to be invoked upon our personal self. The *"boomerang affect"* catches up with us sooner or later. We eventually suffer from the negatives we throw out towards others! The law of sowing and reaping is one we cannot evade.

God consciousness and respect for what he orders and demands is vital to the survival of humankind upon the earth. If we will dedicate ourselves to God's righteous principals, the family of God in the earth can and will survive the test of time and all that it entails! It is our rightful heritage!

Spiritual Stability

We have already pointed out the fact that the family is an ideal ordination of God our Creator. With this thought in mind it should be apparent that the family must stay in communion with the Creator for spiritual nourishment and guidance. Biblical advice from Proverbs 3:5-6, exhorts us:

"To trust the Lord, not our own limited understanding and consult Him for right direction!" (Prov. 3:5-6)

The complex nature of life can only be mastered by a *"Supreme Wisdom"* above that of our own.

When that wisdom is adhered to by family headship the entire family benefits. God who is the source of life and wisdom, imparts that wisdom to man. When man imparts that wisdom to his family and subsequently to each succeeding generation we have the making of strong God fearing families on the earth.

The biblical character, Job, was a devoted family man. It was his dedication to God which caused his family to be blessed. He interceded often to God in behalf of his family. He made positive sacrifices to God.

His life exemplified a moral integrity of righteous character. His spiritual stability was a testimony to his family of what it meant to be a father dedicated to God!

Good Health

Goode health is vital to the longevity of family happiness and overall well being. In these days of *"sky rocketing inflation"* of health care prices, sickness and bad health can impose tremendous hardships on the family budget. Bad health can also hinder the fruitful progression of reproduction of biological offspring. Consequently, if there is no reproduction of human kind the family institution would eventually become distinct.

Job and his companion in matrimony were able to reproduce their kind in multiple measure due to the quality of their biological fitness. To this union ten healthy children were born. What a testimony to their fitness, and what a contribution to the propagation of human kind! What an act of obedience to the Lord's command to: *"be fruitful and multiply!"*

Good health contributes to the strength of the family unit. It provides an opportunity for wholesome family recreation and uninhibited family fellowship! Good mental and physical health are both affected by the spirit of man. Being sick in spirit can negatively influence physical health. When the spirit and body aligns with God's Will the end results culminates in prosperity of body and soul. (See John 3:2-4). When the overall family structure is influenced by submission to biblical principles the whole being of family structure is enhanced and preserved.

Financial Stability

"A feast is made for laughter, and wine maketh merry, but money answereth all things." (Ecc. 10:19

Money is one of those carnal commodities necessary to enhance the comfort of living. Without it in today's society living would be extremely difficult, to say the least! Money is a valuable medium of exchange when utilized constructively and can create wealth of positive maintenance and material attainment. When the material aspect is balanced by spiritual excellence the abundant life for family living prevails.

Many marriages have succumbed do to a lack of financial security or unwise financial investments. The whole family suffers mentally and physically when financial resources are in disarray. A lack of wise financial planning ultimately leads to frustration that Satan can use as a tool to cause a husband and wife conflict over financial matters. If the family is to maintain a level of good financial balance it should always put God first by sharing 10% of the family income to the ministry of the Lord's work!

MAN'S INHERITANCE

The fountains mingle with the river,
And the rivers with the ocean,
The winds of heaven mix forever
With a sweet emotion;
Nothing in the world is single;
ALL things by law divine
In one another's being mingle;
Why not I with thine?
See the mountains kiss high heaven,
And the waves claps one another;
No sister flower would be forgiven
If it disdained it's brother;
And the sunlight clogs the earth,
And the moonbeams kiss the sea;
What are all these kisses worth,
If thou kiss not me?

-Percy Byshe Shelly

DR. EDDIE JERNAGIN

Chapter Four

SINGLENESS AND MARRIAGE

There are numerous opinions when it comes to the subject of being single or married. On occasion I have heard those dissatisfied with marriage admonish the single individual to avoid matrimony. I have heard some that are single express their negative ramifications of singleness.

Being married or single is a fact of life's heritage God wants us to enjoy. Both are honorable states of being. Happiness should not be predicated solely upon one being married or not. The joy of life in great measure has to do with what you think of yourself, your relationship with God, who is your maker and your attitude about personal relationships and life in general.

Singleness is a blessed heritage every human being is blessed to experience. What one does with the direction of their single heritage influences greatly it's enjoyable fulfillment. When a single individual dedicates him or herself to constructive projects to occupy their time, long days and months become filled with constructive activity eliminating the need for someone else to make their life happy! One's involvement in noble activity psychologically makes the length of those days and months not so long down and out after all!

Singleness has it's advantages in that you can devote more attention to the business of the Lord with less distraction than that of a married individual. (see 1 Corin. 7:32-33) Singleness gives you the liberty to come and go at your leisure. Not having the heavy financial responsibility of raising a family is also an advantages aspect of being single.

If you are single you should never base the totality of your happiness upon someone else coming into your life to make it happy. Singleness is a gift from God; life starts out that way! It should be enjoyed to the fullest while you can! If you are the marrying kind it will come at an appointed time. Be happy until it comes!

If you are married be happy and thankful for this spiritual institution. I use the term spiritual because the marital bond is a bonding of two individual spirits becoming as one. Marriage is meant to be much more than a physical connection. The spiritual connection is much stronger than the carnal flesh connection. When two hearts are united as one each individual must cling to that one heart for the survival of spiritual union.

God has said:

"It is not good that man should be alone; I will make him a help mate..." (Genesis 2:18)

As a gift of human heritage the marital bond became honorably bestowed upon man and woman to jointly exchange intellectual, physical and moral communication. The joy of marital union is inherent in the fact that two have merged as one. When a mutual exchange of intellectual, physical and moral communication is shared it should be done in such an unselfish fashion that both parties are happy to make each other happy.

The inherent happiness of the marital union is that of being able to birth and raise a family that characterizes both husband and wife in physical, spiritual and moral excellence. As both parents set the righteous example for their offspring to imitate, the positive image of the marital union is upheld in the reflective character of their offspring. This within itself testifies of the blessed state of the marital bond. Marriage is such an honorable estate until the church is symbolized as the bride of Christ. Just as Christ is protective of His bride, the church, so should a man be protective of his bride, his beloved wife. The church stands on the solid foundation of her groom who is Christ the Son of the living God. The word of God declares:

"The gates of hell shall not prevail against it." (Matthew 16:18)

A married man should be such a strong, vital, loving and caring husband for his wife until the painful challenges of marriage cannot survive against the strength of their marital bond.

The Sex Drive

Christians must not be ashamed or afraid to deal with the subject of sex! The sexual drive is a biological function which is an innate fact of life. It is an inborn drive designed to be shared by those who qualify as a result of marital union. Unfortunately, it is one of those functions in life which has been grossly misused, misunderstood and utilized too often to the point of obsessional extremes. It is one of those functions which can produce an ultimate time of enjoyment or regret depending upon the motivational circumstances behind its use.

For married persons sexual intercourse is one of the greatest physical expressions of interchange. There is no greater gift of physical exchange between husband and wife that can be jointly shared.

It is a sharing and giving in pleasure of biological energy and a spiritual expression of love to each other. Basically, it's fundamental function is for reproductive purposes in accordance to scriptural ordination. God said:

"Be fruitful, multiply and replenish the earth." (Genesis 1:28)

Secondarily, the sexual act is an expression of interchange of physical pleasure. However, it should never be done outside the context of matrimonial bond. When it is done outside of authentic love it becomes a carnal experience against divine approval. If sexual intercourse is committed outside of the marital bond between singles it becomes the sin of fornication. If sexual intercourse is exercised by one who is married with another married participant who legally is married to another person it is the sin of adultery. Married or single learn to enjoy your inheritance of life by serving the Lord who is *"The way, the truth and life."*

(St. John 14:6)

Chapter Five

ABRAHAM'S INHERITANCE

Inheritance in a general sense is usually thought of in its relationship to one becoming an heir of something material and tangible. But inheritance in the sacred scriptures not only involves acquiring physical properties, but encompasses in a broader realm the inheritance of spiritual properties as well.

In the Old Testament we see in operation the prophetic promise of God to Abraham and his descendants relating to the land of Canaan, and all its fruitful blessings. While the operation and purpose of inheritance in the New Testament is connected with the person and work of Jesus Christ. Through the redemptive work of the Master, baptized believers become the Sons of

God by spiritual adoption, and joint heirs with Christ.

Prior to 2100 B.C., God chose the patriarch Abraham and called him out of the land of Ur. It was the Lord's redemptive purpose to bring Abram into a saving covenant with himself and to make Abraham's seed a nation in Palestine, through which some day, salvation would be brought to the entire world.

Abraham's relationship with God was a remarkable one indeed. In this relationship there were several important factors in operation: 1) The Divine Call of God; 2) The prophetic promises of God; 3) the steadfast faith of Abraham.

> **1) The Divine Call**
> *"Now the Lord has said unto Abram, get thee out of thy country, and from they father's house, unto a land that I will show thee." (Genesis 12:1)*

The Divine Call of God involves a special choice of a chosen human vessel to carry out God's Divine Master plan on the earth.

The chosen individual usually possesses unique qualities which distinguishes him from others. He is given divine direction and empowered by God to accomplish His Divine Will. Such was the case with Abraham.

It might be well to point out that one's comprehension of divine directives is not always immediately clear. But humility and obedience to the Divine Call is paramount, if the one who is called expects to be blessed.

Abraham obeyed the Divine Call and the directions of God which eventually led to his blessings. Also, thousands of others became recipients of God's blessings and favors because of Abraham's obedience. Abraham was without a doubt a chosen reservoir through which all families of the earth became blessed.

Down through the corridors of Biblical history the Divine Call of God was heeded by dedicated men who though their obedience to God's call upon their life contributed greatly to the inherited blessings of countless millions in human history.

The great Hebrew prophets of antiquity as Isaiah, Jeremiah, Malachi and Micah all heedfully accepted the Divine beckoning to fulfill the prophetic office. Boldly speaking forth the divine oracles of Elohim (God the strong one) through which the movements of all history past, present and future inevitable parallel.

There are those who say that God does not call men today, but this writer is inclined to believe that He still calls today.

The Bible profoundly proclaims that God *"is the same yesterday, today and forever."*

"Then said I, woe is me. For I am undone; because I am a man of unclean lips, and I dwell in the midst of a people of unclean lips, for mine eyes have seen the King, the Lord of Hosts.

Then flew one of the seraphims unto me, having a live coal in his hand, which he had taken with the tongs from off the alter;

And he laid it upon my mouth, and said, Lo, this hath touched thy lips, and thine iniquity is taken away, and thy sin purged.

And I heard the voice of the lord, saying, whom shall I send, and who will go for us!

Then said I, here am I, send me! *(Isa.6:5-8)*

2) Prophetic Promises to Abraham

"And I will make of thee a great nation, and I will bless thee, and make thy name great, and thou shalt be a blessing. And I will bless them that bless thee, and curse him that curseth thee, and in thee

shall all families of the earth be blessed." (Genesis 12:2-3)

Abraham was placed in the unique position of becoming the central figure through which a great nation would have its origin. The Divine covenant bestowed upon Abraham, though challenged by the strong forces of Israel's adversaries, remained firm in spite of intensive opposition, because of God's unparalleled love for His chosen people.

The nation of Israel descended from Abraham as God had emphatically promised. And to the amazement of her adversaries and allies alike, she stands today as an envied territory testifying to the fulfillment of the unwavering promise of Jehovah!

The blessings bestowed upon Abraham were multiple. He was a wealthy man during his lifetime. This can be attributed to his loyal devotion to God, and also to the faithfulness of God's promise that he would be blessed. From the inception of the Abrahamic Covenant to the dispensation of grace, Jews and Christians alike, as well as all the families of the earth have been blessed!

God vowed to bless those that would bless Abraham and his offspring. And also to curse those who cursed them. A review of history will vividly reveal the destruction or decline of those who have chosen to inflict oppression and gross adversity towards Israel, such as Egypt, Babylon, Persia, Assyria, Napoleon's France, Hitler's Germany, etc..

The Divine Covenants of God have been proven through generations to be steadfast and sure! In contrasting comparison the promises of treaties of fallen mankind are often broken! With whom will you choose to confide?

3) The Faith of Abraham

"And he believed in the Lord, and he counted it to him for righteousness."

(Genesis 15:6)

So numerous and fantastic were the promises which God made to Abraham that it would require childlike faith (believing without seeing) on the behalf of Abraham to look steadfastly towards the future to such unprecedented promises becoming a reality.

Abraham's Milestone

Abraham's first milestone of trust of God's promises was expressed when he chose to leave his father's habitation for a strange land he had never seen.

"Abram took Sarai his wife, and Lot his brother's son, and all their substance that they had gathered, and the souls that they had gotten in Haran, and they went forth to go into the land of Canaan"(Genesis 12:5)

Time after time the Great God Jehovah renewed his covenant to encourage Abram's faith.

As a result of each inherited blessing Abraham received, his faith in God's Word was also strengthened. He had only to look back in his past to see positive confirmation of God's infallible promises. This, in turn, gave him added confidence to believe for future conquests.

Abraham's Challenge

One of the most challenging experiences to Abraham's faith occurred when God asked him to offer his son as a human sacrifice for a burnt offering.

Undoubtedly, the question came to Abraham's mind- *"God, why my own flesh and blood?"* Nevertheless, in spite of his depth of tender fatherly love for his son, Isaac, his faith motivated by love for God abounded!

"Isaac spake unto Abraham, his father, and said, My father, and he said, here am I my son. And he said, Behold the wood, But where is the lamb for a burnt offering? And Abraham said, My son, God will provide himself a lamb for a burnt offering." (Genesis 22:7-8)

In the preceding scriptural quotation one can see Abraham's faith responding to his son's probing inquisitiveness.

With such faith being exemplified on Abraham's behalf Jehovah God could not resist coming to Abraham's aid during the confrontation of the challenge. Faith in God always reciprocates God's favor!

"And the angel of the Lord called unto him out of heaven, and said, Abraham, Abraham, and he said, Here am I. And he said, Lay not thine hand upon the lad, neither do thou anything, unto him. For now I know that thou fearest God, seeing thou hast not withheld they son, thine only son from me." (Genesis 22:12)

Man Needs A Challenge

I am prone to believe it is the will of God for certain situations to confront mankind in life that will require a releasing of one's faith for deliverance. Even though many times we do not understand God's way of doing certain things,

"...all things work together for good to them that love God..." (Romans 8:28)

Let us now praise famous men,

Our fathers in their generation's

The Lord manifested in them a great glory,

Even his mighty power from the beginning.

Such as did bear rule in their Kingdoms,

And were men renowned for their power,

Giving counsel by their understanding,

Such as have brought tiding in prophecies:

Leaders of the people by their counsels.

Excerpts from "Our Fathers"

By Jesus Sirach

Chapter Six

GOD AND THE ISRAELITES

History cannot ignore man's relationship with his creator. History begins with God who is *"The Beginning"* and it will close with the final acts of God who is *"The Ending."*

God controls history, and His master plan of events past, present, and future are precisely under His control, in spite of the rebellious profile of human history.

Historically, it has been the compassionate aim of God to bring his people into the fullness of their predestined inheritance.

This is clearly obvious with His dealings with the Israelites under the Old Covenant, as well as his dealing with the Jews, and spiritual Israel today (converted Christian believers of all races and nations).

God has always heard the cry of His children. He has also seen the gross injustices imposed upon them by enviable men.

Ultimately however, the strong (committed believers) will survive and inherit all that has been Divinely promised throughout the limitless span of eternity!!

The Call of Moses

From the back side of a serene desert place, to the forefront of human history, Moses was called on to assume a unique position of leadership. Commissioned by the Great God of Abraham, Isaac, and Jacob with the awesome assignment of standing before the Egyptian Pharaoh to demand the deliverance of Israel out of bondage.

Moses being a humble inarticulate sheepherder felt within himself to be quite unqualified for such an unprecedented major venture. This, in the overall analysis of what was to transpire, proved to be one of his chief assets because it was characteristic of God to use humble men.

Along with Jehovah, Moses and his spokesman, Aaron, the threesome became an unbeatable trio. In the midst of what seemed to have been staggering odds, the promised land *"flowing with milk and honey"* became their destined pursuit.

Big Men Fall Hard

Pharaoh, possessing royal authority deemed it unacceptable to yield to the firm demand of Jehovah. His stubbornness and blind ignorance of God set the stage for one of the great confrontations of mortal man's pride and rebellion opposing the Omnipotent Dynamism of the Lord! Of course, Pharaoh's resistance proved to be fruitless, and God abounded! Reluctantly, after untold suffering and embarrassment, the grievous loss of his beloved firstborn son, and overall defeat, the Egyptian Pharaoh released God's children. Not until the dramatic encounter with the power of God at the Red Sea did his reneging efforts finally succumb.

As the children of Israel marched towards freedom, little did they realize what was to transpire in the trying days ahead. Meanwhile, back in the adobe of Pharaoh, preparation was being made once again to openly defy the stern command of God. Like a raving mad man yearning for revenge, Pharaoh ordered the armed forces of Egypt to overtake the children of God.

God's children had hardly begun to inhale the sweet fragrance of freedom when in the far distance the intensive thundering of hoofs could be heard pounding against the hot desert sands. Vague mushroom-like clouds of dust could be seen through the denseness of dusk, billowing from the floor of the parched earth, as the rumbling sounds of rushing chariot wheels of pharaoh's militaristic forces pushed steadily towards their frightened prey with lightning speed.

Hysterically, Jehovah's bewildered children, unable to go forward because of the Red Sea, began to angrily complain to their leader about their plight. Moses, being a man acquainted with pressurizing circumstances which was indicative of his leadership position, exhorted the people to stand firm and witness the works of God which would be manifested in miraculous measure.

As Moses lifted the rod and stretched forth his hand over the water, the Omnipotent Dynamics of the Lord activated the winds' velocity:

> *"And the Lord caused the sea to go back by a strong east wind all that night, and made the sea dry land, and the waters were divided."*

(Exodus 14:21)

Scampering for freedom God's determined children dashed for the distant shore of liberation; while the pursuing forces of pharaoh's hosts bore down upon them. As the last Israelite stumbled ashore, panting for fresh air, Moses again:

"stretched forth his hand over the sea, and the sea returned to his strength when the morning appeared and the Egyptians fled against it; and the Lord overthrew the Egyptians in the midst of the sea. And the waters returned, and covered the chariots, and the horsemen, and all the hosts of Pharaoh that came into the sea after them; there remained not so much as one of them." (Exodus 14:27-28)

While the promised land of milk and honey lay waiting for the Israelites to inherit, they wandered for forty years in the wilderness of despair, rebellion, disobedience and sin!

Thirsting for lack of water, they came to the bitter water of Marah, not suitable for human consumption. Yet God proved himself to be the great I Am once again" by making the bitter waters sweet. Murmuring against Moses and Aaron for want of bread, fresh manna was delivered each morning and in the evening a generous supply of luscious quail was supplied by an intercessory act of God to fulfill their appetite.

Needing Divine laws to be governed by, the Ten Commandments were established as the standard basis upon which men through the lineage of human existence are to govern themselves.

A Type of the Christian Life

The pilgrimage of Israel depicts a type of Christian life. Bound by the bondage of sin Christ came to deliver mankind from the enslavement of sin. The exodus begins the moment the enslaved individual receives by faith the spiritual person of Christ in his heart as Lord and Savior. After deliverance from the bondage of sin, every evil force of the adversary seems to pursue the converted one. Nevertheless, Christ becomes the believers' power. This power in turn brings the believer through the *"Red Sea"* of hindrances. The bitter waters of life's perplexities are miraculously made sweet through the Spirit of Christ. After every bitter experience the hunger of the believer for spiritual manna becomes fulfilled through Jesus who is The Bread of Life!

How exhilarating it must have been for a people who after four-hundred-eighty years of oppressive enslavement to finally gain a new life of freedom. Nevertheless, how painful it is for a people to be delivered from bondage yet because of yielding to the ways of the *"flesh"* nullify the promised inheritance of reaching the land flowing with "milk and honey!" Such was the case of those among the one million Israelites who were delivered from the bondage of Egyptian rule. The vast majority who left Egypt met death in the wilderness because of their defiant attitudes.

I venture to say that millions are dying in bitter despair today that will never reach the richness and beauty of the celestial city (heaven) because of a pessimistic attitude towards the way God intents from men to be spiritually governed. Of the approximate one million or more Israelites who left Egypt, only two of the original hosts set foot upon the Promised Land...Joshua and Caleb? The tenure of Moses as leader of God's children, expired when he reached the golden age of one hundred and twenty years. His comrade and spokesman, Aaron, died at the age of one hundred twenty-three, forty years after the exodus.

A New Leader

The enormous burden of bringing Israel into the Promised Land now became the inherent responsibility of Joshua, who was a most capable young dynamo in his own respect!

Schooled at the feet of his elder, Moses, the transition of leadership could not have been transferred into the hands of a more qualified successor. Joshua had witnessed first hand the devoted fortitude of Moses fulfilling the Divine call even in the heat of monumental odds!

Again, even as with Moses, we see the Divine strategy of Jehovah constructing an avenue for Joshua to lead the new generation of Israelites to victory.

The warfare of Israel actually became the warfare of God, and without the intercessory genius of God Canaan would not have become Israel's inheritance.

*Sound the loud Timbrel o'er Egypt's
dark sea!
Jehovah has triumphed – his people are free.
Sing – for the pride of the Tyrant is
Broken, His chariots, his horsemen,
all splendid and brave –
How vain was their boast, for the
Lord hath but spoken, And chariots
And horsemen are sunk in the wave.
Sound the loud Timbrel o'er Egypt's
dark sea;
Jehovah has triumphed – his people
are free.
Praise to the Conqueror, praise to the
Lord. His word was our arrow,
his breath was our sword.
Who shall return to tell Egypt the story
Of those she sent forth in the hour
of her pride?*

For the Lord hath looked out from his pillar of glory, and all her brave thousands are dashed in the tide. Sound the loud Timbrel o'er Egypt's dark sea! Jehovah has triumphed – his people are free.

Thomas Moore

Chapter 7

GREED FOR MATERIALISM

Unfortunately, too many individuals can see no further than the "tenure" of their existence. In the process of acquiring happiness, building vast empires, and pursuing prosperity for the temporal time of their life, they have not taken time out to consider their eternal existence after the limited time of life is past.

Greed has its origin within the seed of sin. When the seed is nourished within the mind, the possessed individual is then subjected to various thoughts the sinful seed produces. The ideas produced can range anywhere from armed robbery to murder, dope peddling, prostitution, gambling, etc., for the expressed purposed of obtaining material or monetary wealth.

It is little wonder why the Apostle Paul in his letter to Timothy said:

"the love of money is the root of all evil."
(I Timothy 6:10)

The Shame of Greed

The lascivious vice of greed motivates evil men to strategize and destroy their own kind. One basic premise for conflict among nations is a lack of trust and respect for cultural differences, and the inordinate desire to possess wealth of other nations.

An examination of history reveals frightening sketches of shameful periods of terror brought on by selfish men demonically possessed and obsessed with the prideful ambition of becoming the *"supreme"* number one.

The reign of Adolph Hitler, the days of Alexander the Great and the pronouncement of communist dictators to conquer the world reflects the miserable shame of greed. Each period of man's history has seen millions of innocent, law abiding and God loving men slaughtered and maimed because of greed for materialism and political power.

Middle East Wealth

The Middle East is a steady *"boiling point"* of conflict because of agitation, envy and greedy lust of various nations to possess the wealth of natural resources that exist in that part of the world.

"Israel is destined to become a very rich nation. We have all witnesses the fact that wealthy Jews from all over the world, sympathetic toward Israel, have invested millions of capital in that country. She is without doubt the economic marvel of the world, Well-substantiated reports indicate that the extensive engineering study of the mineral resources of the Dead Sea estimated them to be in the vicinity of three trillion dollars at the beginning of this century. Due to inflation they would be worth six to eight trillion dollars today. In addition, she is surrounded by oil-rich countries. Who knows what success the present Israeli oil attempts will produce!" Her enemies stand ready to devour her riches at any cost!

The following scripture is an overview of the prophetic discourse of Ezekiel as he describes the end-time Russian invasion of Israel which shall be prompted by greed:

"Thou shalt ascent and come like a storm, thou shalt be like a cloud to cover the land, thou, and all thy bands and many people with thee.

Thus sayeth the Lord God, it shall also come to pass that at the same time, shall things come into thy mind, and thou shall think an evil thought: And thou shalt say, I will go up to the unwalled villages; I will go to them that are at rest, that dwell safely, all of them dwelling without walls, and having neither bars nor gates,

To take a spoil, and to take a prey; to turn thine hand upon the desolate places that are now inhabited, and upon the people that are gathered out of the nations, which have gotten cattle and goods, that dwell in the midst of the land." (Ezekiel 38:9-12)

Sacred Holidays Diluted

The spiritual significance of our religious holidays, such as Easter, Thanksgiving and Christmas have been drastically diminished because of the greed of money hungry merchants to secure record financial gains, and by the lust of consumers to enhance their already bulging wardrobes and gadgetry collections.

The bunny rabbit, the beautiful bonnet, and the flamboyant pastel frock seem to dominate the Easter scene, rather than the glorious resurrection of our Lord.

Thanksgiving is generally a day of gross gluttony where the stomachs of millions are stuffed to the point of greedy sin. Grandmother's delicious turkey and dressing, topped by her scrumptious pumpkin pie is the topic of praise, rather than giving thanks to God and compassionate benevolence to the underprivileged.

Christmas, in this era of greed, call for the promotion of jolly old Santa Claus and Rudolph, the Red Nosed Reindeer. Millions of dollars are spent for fashionable advertising to lure the public into buying gifts, while the all-important birth of Christ, for which this day should be ordained to honor, plays *"second fiddle"* in the minds of millions!

In man's quest for political power, earthly prestige, material wealth, and worldly fame, he fails to realize that these *"now"* ecstasies will perish with time. The only thing that will stand the test of time and eternity will be what he has done for the kingdom of God in Christ upon this earth.

That does not mean that there is no place for the political arena or materialism in the *"now"* of our worldly existence. We do, indeed, live in a physical world that requires physical matter and political function, but when these earthly matters obstruct our spiritual vision and responsibility to God, they damn us! Thus, when this life has expired we have no eternal inheritance of *"life"* with Christ, but death, which is the ultimate finality of greed!

The Lord is not opposed to men having riches. It is his will that men be: 1) happy *"now"* 2) enjoy life *"now"* 3) have food in the refrigerator *"now"* 4) have money in their pocket *"now"* and 5) have an abundant life upon earth *"now"*. However, one's aspiration should not be based solely upon the *"now"* of existence, but more so in a broader spectrum inclusive of the *"now"* of life, as well as the eternal!

MAN'S INHERITANCE

Use your money while you're living,
Do not hoard it to be proud;
You can never take it with you –
There's no pocket in a shroud.
Gold can help you on no further,
Than the graveyard where you lie,
And though you are rich while living,
You're a pauper when you die.
Use it then to brighten some lives,
As through life they weary plod;
Place your bank account in heaven
And grow richer toward your God.
Use it wisely, use it freely,
Do not hoard it to be proud;
You can never take it with you –
There's no pocket in a shroud.

- Author Unknown

DR. EDDIE JERNAGIN

Chapter Eight

DETERMINATION

When a man yields his life and ways to God he steps out of death into eternal life. He also has total access through faith to the unlimited treasures of his Supreme Creator. Whether he receives these riches or not depends upon his faith and determination to obtain his inheritance in the midst of satanic opposition.

Perhaps, you have heard the proverb, *"Where there's a will, there's a way."* I, as a minister of the gospel of Jesus Christ, have found this wise saying to be very true indeed. However, whether one's will develops into a living reality depends on his determination to achieve his goal, no matter what the price or sacrifice. There are many sincere Christians who have visions and dreams of doing bigger and better things for the cause of Christ on earth, but, somewhere along life's way, they become weak and discouraged by the challenge to their determination to do great things for God.

It is a pertinent fact that as a result of fear and the lack of faith many of God's people are afraid to make new resolutions to do greater things for God. They fear that if they make a vow they may not keep it, or if they set a goal they may not be successful in their attempts to reach their goal. With this particular attitude and outlook, one is defeated before he begins because the devil has set up fear in the mind. The only way to eradicated this tormenting fear is to set your goal and be determined that with the help of the Almighty, *"I'm going to reach my goal!"*

When the goal for attaining greater heights and depths in the will of God is established, it gives you something to reach for in your spiritual life. Furthermore, it motivates you out of a *"do nothing"* attitude into an active warrior for the Lord. It brings you out of the state of being just a "bench warmer" in the church into an active soldier for Christ.

In military service, men are prepared to go into combat against an enemy with the purpose of winning the battle. Many are wounded and slain, but the battle goes on with those who remain with a determination to inherit victory. So it is in God's army, we are in this battle to win!

The mountain climber faces the challenge of reaching the mountain peak and he gets tired and weary, but he keeps on climbing, because he's determined to reach the top. Are you determined to reach the top of the mountain for Christ and receive your inheritance?

I am reminded of a story I once heard from a fellow minister telling of the epic journey of two adventurers trying to conquer the dangerous slopes of a rugged mountain. One of the men had reached the top of the peak, but his companion was struggling to reach the top by clinging to a rope. In the process of climbing, the rope got caught in a cluster of branches and he was unable to free himself by hand.

He then took out his knife and attempted to cut the branches, but in the process of doing so, he accidentally snagged the rope with his razor sharp knife, and the weight of his body was about to break the rope. So there he was, hundreds of feet above ground level but just a few feet from the top of the mountain with his life hanging in the balance. In a desperate attempt to save himself, he yelled hysterically for advice from his friend who had already reached the top. Then, in the echoes of wholesome instruction which came from his friend, he heard him say these lifesaving words, *"reach above the cut place!"* He did exactly that and it saved his life. Thus, with his determination to reach the top of the mountain, he continued to climb, ultimately reaching his destined goal.

In your attempts to reach the top of the mountain for God, your spiritual line may be cut, but take the advice of those who have made it to the top, *"Reach above the cut place!"* "Reach above your fears!" *"Reach above your doubt!" "Reach above the failures of your past!" "Reach above your foe!" "Be determined to conquer the challenge, make your life count for God and claim your inherited blessing!"* Let God be magnified above our challenging circumstances!

It is a typical tactic of the enemy to: 1) hinder your progress in God in any way he can, 2) break down your determination, 3) make you fear setting spiritual goals and 4) make you an inactive Christian. However, be determined to defeat him and win the race! Furnish the will and determination and God will make the way. He is unequivocally, your God and your *"Way!"*

Jacob's encounter with an angelic being brought an inherited blessing as a result of his determined efforts to obtain deliverance from death at the hands of his brother Esau:

"And Jacob was left alone, and there wrestled a man with him until the breaking of the day.

And when he saw that he prevailed not against him, he touched the hollow of his thigh, and the hollow of Jacob's thigh was out of joint as he wrestled with him.

And he said let me go, for the day breaketh. And he said, I will not let thee go, except thou bless me. And he said unto him, what is thy name? And he said, Jacob.

And he said, thy name shall be called no more Jacob, but Israel. For as a prince, has thou power with God and with men, and he prevailed." (Genesis 32:24-28)

You, too can inherit power and favor with God in your life today. As His child, you have become an heir adopted into the Royal Family. However, one must realize to retain the spiritual benefits of this Royal adoption and to obtain greater spiritual heights, one must have the determination of Jacob, the faith of Abraham and the integrity of Job!

The harder the thing is to do,

DR. EDDIE JERNAGIN

The greater the joy when it's done,

The farther the goal is from you,

The sweeter the thrill when it's won.

The deeper the problem,

The more is the joy when you've

Puzzled it out;

The seas that run farthest from shore,

Are only for ships that are stout.

Men weary of lessons they've learned,

And tire of the tasks they can do.

Life it seems is forever concerned

With blazing a path to the new.

So stand to the worry and care.

Everlastingly keep going on.

The greater the burden you bear,

The greater the joy when it's done.

Author Unknown

Chapter Nine

INHERITING RICHES THROUGH THANKSGIVING & PRAISE

Enter into His gates with thanksgiving, and into His courts with praise, be thankful unto Him, and bless His name.
(Psalms 100:4)

Have you ever stopped to consider your blessing as opposed to our trials, tribulations and misfortunes? If not, stop reading this book for just a few moments and review your lifetime upon this earth. Sure, you have perhaps suffered defeats during the years, but just think back from whence God has brought you.

I have found when I have a tendency to feel sorry for myself or begin to worry about tomorrow's problems, a soothing voice whispers to me and says, "Look from where I have brought you in the past, give thanks, and take courage to believe that if I made a way for you in the past, I shall do so in the future." It is then I begin to give thanks and praise to God, and many times to my delightful amazement, that which I desired to have, becomes my inheritance.

As an evangelist minister, I have discovered two things to be of paramount value in enjoying the goodness of life, and in obtaining things from God to meet the needs and desires of my heart. They are *"faith"* and *"thanksgiving."*

One's faith in God brings about that which one asks of Him. Extending praises and thanksgiving to God delights the heart of the Almighty. It also creates a positive atmosphere for your faith to bask within. Therefore, two of the most relevant keys to receiving the choice benefits of God's blessings are to praise His name and be thankful for that which he has already bestowed upon you.

There have been times when I felt low in spirit, frustrated and discouraged. But I have learned that by exercising faith and expressions of sincere gratitude during the challenge of such adverse conditions the mind gradually becomes cleared of negative thoughts, which in turn help to alleviate the inherent pain in the problem. Try praising and thanking God in the time of adverse confrontations, and witness the amazing favorable returns!

Thanksgiving and adoration unto the Lord elevates the mind to a *"glory realm"* where pain cannot penetrate. Giving praise is a spiritual experience which ushers you into God's presence, where supernatural strength and victory is assured!

In the book of II Chronicles, the twentieth chapter, there is an amazing episode. King Jehoshaphat of Judah was facing adverse circumstances. It would require a miracle from God to deliver he and the children of Judah from the hands of the enemy who pursued them with utter destruction of Judah in mind! The odds were overwhelmingly stacked against Judah! They had neither the manpower nor the weapons to retaliate against the allied armies that came against them. But, thanks be to God, even in the midst of what seemed to be sure defeat for Jehoshaphat and his small band of followers, the Almighty God gave them the victory because they praised the *"beauty of holiness,"* even though they were going through an astonishing period of trial!

"And when he (King Jehoshaphat) had consulted with the people, he appointed singers unto the Lord, and that they should praise the

beauty of holiness, as they went out before the army, and to say, praise the Lord, for his mercy endureth forever. And when they began to sing and to praise, the Lord set ambushments against the children of Ammon, Moab and Mount Seir, which were come against Judah, and they were smitten." (II Chronicles 20:21-22)

I venture to say that many are living beneath their privilege and missing the riches of God because they fail to praise Him in their time of adversity.

Jehoshaphat and his small band of followers not only received the victory over the adversary through their praises to God, but the Lord also made them literally wealthy, as a result of *"praising the beauty of holiness."*

"And when Judah came toward the watch tower in the wilderness, they looked unto the multitude, and behold there were dead bodies fallen to the earth, and more escaped.

"And when Jehoshaphat and his people came to take away the spoil of them, they found among them in abundance both riches with the dead bodies, and precious jewels, which they stripped off for themselves, more than they could carry away, and they were three days in gathering of the spoil, it was so much." (II Chronicles 20:24-25)

You, too can receive an abundant inheritance of joy and riches by praising and thanking the Divine Creator. He has delivered you in the past, even unto this present moment. Lift your hands and praise Him, now!

Thank God for Life!
Even though it bring much bitterness and strife.
And all our fairest hopes be wrecked and lost,
Even though there be more ill than good in life,
We cling to life and reckon not the cost.
Thank God for life! Thank God for love!
For though sometimes grief follows in its wake,
Still we forget love's sorrow in love's joy,
And cherish tears with smile
For love's dear sake;
Only in heaven is bliss without alloy.
Thank God for love! Thank God for pain!
No tear hath ever yet been shed in vain,
No curse, but blessings in hand of pain;
Even when He smiteth,
Then is God most kind.
Thank God for pain! Thank God for death!
Who touches anguished lips and stills their breath
And giveth peace unto each troubled breast;

Grief flies before they touch, O blessed death;
God's sweetest gift, they name in heaven is Rest.
Thank God for death!

(Author Unknown)

DR. EDDIE JERNAGIN

Chapter Ten

THE BIBLE (GOD'S WORD)

While relaxing one evening listening to a *"talk show"* over the radio, the host was asking his listening audience to call into the broadcasting station and share their personal opinion on the colloquial term *"soul food."*

He received such responsive answers as turnip greens and salt pork, cornbread and chitterlings, pigs feet and cabbage, pork chops and pinto beans, etc. I found the answers to be quite amusing. But the response which impressed me most of all came from a gentleman of Christian faith who stated that his definition of *"soul food"* was *"reading the word of God (the Bible) and digesting its contents."*

Upon hearing that response, immediately the scriptural passage came to my mind which states that *"man shall not live by bread alone, but by every word that proceedeth out of the mouth of God." (Matthew 4:4)*

Incomparable

The Bible (God's Word) is by far the most amazing book ever written! No other literary volume in human history has stirred so much controversy among men as to its interpretation and authenticity.

It is a perennial best seller filled with gross excitement and drama that will stimulate the most stagnant mind! It is without question a fascinating book of life!

Within the sacred confines of the Bible the probing mind discovers the explosive revelation of the infinite mind of God.

There is little wonder that finite minds are filled with awe as to the profound creativity, wisdom, wrath and compassion that is unveiled in the Word of God.

Unlike ordinary prose which is matter-of-fact and commonplace, God's word is Divinely inspired, which makes the depth of its profound revelations incomprehensible to the wisest scholars and intellectuals, yet very meaningful to *"babes"* (humble men who choose to have child-like faith in God)

"I thank thee O Father, Lord of heaven and earth, that thou hast hid these things from the wise and prudent, and revealed them to babes" *(St. Luke 20:21)*

Contrasting Viewpoints

Between the seventeenth and nineteenth centuries the progressiveness of science and modern Biblical scholarship raised new challenges to Bible interpretation.

Astronomers, geologists and biologists introduced a contrasting view of the universe from that of the Bible. Intellectual scholars argued that the original sacred writings had undergone diverse alterations, thereby casting doubt upon the literary and traditional authorship of the Biblical books. During the latter part of the nineteenth century the intellectual temper regarded the message of the Bible as somewhat irrelevant to modern times.

The resulting effect of the new studies suggests that the Bible is not the unaltered Word of God, but rather an historical conditioned account of mankind's quest for God. The Roman Catholic Church first declared heretical those results of historical and scientific research that undermined traditional church teaching. Later, under Pius XII (r. 1939-1958) it offered encouragement to research, declaring that the results, if true, would not vary from the traditions and dogma of the church. But to Protestants, who considered the Bible the center of their faith, the new studies were a considerable blow.

Protestants have since split into two theological camps. Fundamentalists maintain the literal truth of the Bible, and do not accept any Biblical or scientific studies that contradict the Biblical word.

Other Protestants, particularly the theologians and scholars, known as high critics, are leaders in the new critical studies." 1

Morality Concepts

Before moral codes can be established, there must be an authoritative basis from which moral and civic laws can derive. The Bible's influence upon the Judeo-Christian concept provides unparalleled vital information from which high moral concepts have derived.

It is only when men choose to deviate from the strong divine commands of God that the fiber of great nations decay. We have but to look in retrospect to the great world empires of the past, and the America of today for an example of gross erosion of high standards of morality because of moral degradation, and complete disrespect for God's moral laws projected within the Bible.

The Ten Commandments

Out of the righteousness and purity of God's being has come the explicit command of the Ten Commandments. Mankind is the direct object in whom the Holy Commandments have been addressed. Yet, from the mouth of fallen man one often hears it said that it is impossible in our society to uphold the Ten Commandments.

If this, indeed, is true, God's Commands would be useless, null and void, and not worthy of being recorded within the Bible. However, the fact of the matter is, selfish mankind rejects the Creator's demands thereby blinding themselves, which makes it difficult for men to believe the Ten Commandments can be strictly adhered to.

God does not waste words, nor back down on his commands! Jehovah emphatically states:

"So shall my word be that goeth forth out of my mouth, it shall not return unto me void, but it shall accomplish that which I please, and shall prosper in the things whereto I sent it. " (Isa. 66:11)

It is impossible to govern one's self by the Ten Commandments only when trying to do it in self-reliance without God's Holy spirit living *"The Life"* within. God's nature living *"The Life"* in the soul of man is put into operation when the soul yields its total person by faith in God's care and profound truth! The Commandments were written in the Holy book to be strictly adhered. God never commands that which he knows is impossible to do. All his demands are within reason!

The Prophets Speak

The prophets were by no means ordinary in the simple sense of the word *"ordinary."* A study of the long and short range prophesies will attest to that fact! It is true that they were ordinary men in their physical person, but used extensively in a supernatural capacity when moved upon, and inspired by the Holy spirit to speak forth prophetic utterances.

To see unfolding before our very eyes the fulfillment of the prophets predictions forecast centuries ago with no iota of deviation; who can honestly say, and show clear cut facts that the Bible is not the inspired Word of God?

Invincible Fortress

The Bible and its doctrinal principles have been the tested target upon which verbal assaults have been targeted, and the spring board from which denominations claim to have sprung.

Without equal, it has been the foremost read literary documentation ever written. Therefore, it is easy to see why one could not be considered fully educated in the stricter sense until a general knowledge of biblical events and principles have been attained and explored through personal exposure.

In spite of the venomous skepticism of the unbelievers in its authenticity, the Bible lives on as a monument of hope for the faithful, who chose to cling to its sacred hinges.

It is strong and can never be destroyed! It is more than rhythmical verses— it is God!:

"And the Word was with God, and the Word was God." (St. John 1:1)

The Holy Scriptures contain sound doctrinal trueness and righteous principles of character which liberates the soul of fallen men out of bondage!

"Ye shall know the truth, and the truth shall make you free!" (St. John 8:32)

The Word of God is Life!

"In Him (Jesus – The Living Word) was life, and the life was the light of men." (St. John 1:4)

The Bible is Divine Law!

"The law of the Lord is perfect, converting the soul..." (Psalms 19:7)

God's Word is Eternal!

"The grass withereth, the flower fadeth, but the word of our God shall stand forever!" (Isa. 40:8)

MAN'S INHERITANCE

It is the Invincible Fortress!

This, my dear friend, Is your inheritance!

Study it carefully, think of it prayerfully,

Deep in thy heart,

Let its pure precepts dwell!

Slight not its history,

Ponder its mystery,

None can e're prize it too fondly or well.

Accept the glad tidings,

The warning and chidings,

Found in his volume of heavenly lore;

With faith that's unfailing,

And love all prevailing,

Trust in its promise of life evermore.

With fervent devotion,

And thankful emotion,

Hear the blest welcome, respond to its call;

Life's purest oblation,

The heart's adorations

Give to the Savior who dies for us all.

May this message of love,

From this tribune above,

To all nations and kindreds be given,

Till the ransomed shall rise

Joyous anthem of praise –

Hallelujah! On earth and in heaven!

Author Unknown

Chapter Eleven

INHERITANCE OF LOVE

The supreme passion in life is Love! It is the motivating force behind the miracle of existence of all things created. The Holy Scriptures proclaim that:

God is love. And in the beginning of time Love said, *"let there be – and there was…"*

Human rebellion created a huge gulf between God and man, in spite of this, the Creator so loved His creation that he was passionately willing to sacrifice His only Son to bridge the dangerous gap which the destructiveness of sin had brought into being. For decades men have been benefactors of this unsurmountable Divine expression.

Love in the genuine sense is not merely the expression of a kiss upon the cheek of another. It might be well to point out that it was a kiss placed upon the person of Jesus by Judas which eventually led to His capture and crucifixion.

Love is not merely the giving of a delectable, tangible gift. Gifts can often be given in order to receive a gift in exchange. Love is not merely the exchange of sexual energy between a man and a woman, because this act is often committed not in accord with love, but rather lustful passion. However, this is not to say that sexual expression is wrong. It is, indeed, a beautiful experience when committed in accord with God's ordination.

Love is not merely poetic verse uttered with polished eloquence by an articulate poet. Love is not merely a smile, a handshake, or a compliment exchanged by individuals during the course of interchanging communication. Too often this is done in hypocrisy.

Love is the expressed cry of Jesus saying,

"Father forgive them for they know not what they do."

As He hung on the cross bearing our gross sins in His body. Yes, again it merits repeating, *"God is Love!"* The ultimate test of His love was fulfilled in the brutal death of His beloved son for the atoning of humanity's unrighteousness.

"For God so loved the world that He gave His only begotten Son" (St. John 3:16)

"Greater love hath no man than this, that a man lay down his life for his friends." (St. John 15:13)

A New Breed

When Jesus came upon the scene of time in his physical being, the world beheld a new breed of man. One who not only emphatically preached love, but applied every principle of love in His own personal mode of living. He practiced passive resistance even in the face of death, when He could have called upon the entire angelic host to fortify His innocence. He exhorted his followers to love their enemies, and do good to them who would despitefully use them:

"And unto him smiteth thee on the one cheek offer also the other, and him that taketh away thy cloak forbid not to take thy coat also." (St. Luke 6:29)

It is little wonder that the multitudes who heard the Master teach were confounded at such a profound philosophy. Many of his day were bound by tradition under the Law. Therefore, instead of loving their antagonists, they chose rather to retaliate according to customs of past traditionalism.

It is an impossibility for a man to love in the true sense of love if he has not accepted God in Christ as his savior. For how can one love if he does not possess the basis from which compassion is conceived – God?

The Almighty has directed intimate affection toward that which he has created in His likeness – man. We are the chief beneficiaries in whom His love is directed. If we have accepted him, the manifestation of all the principles Christ applied must also operate in us.

Spiritually speaking, it is not we who love our enemy, for our nature rebels against it. But it is the love of Christ abounding in the heart that motivates one to love as He has commanded:

"But love ye your enemies, and do good, and lend, hoping for nothing again, and your reward (inheritance) shall be great, and ye shall be the children of the highest, for he is kind unto the thankful and to the evil. " (St. Luke 6:35)

Moved by Compassion

The compassion which Jesus possessed motivated Him to meet the needs of those with whom He came into contact. There is no great mystery as to why he attracted the poor, needy and rejected. These were individuals deprived of compassion because of their social status. They could not communicate their grievances and needs effectively with the *"upper establishment."* But when they came to Jesus He took time to listen and was moved with compassion to touch them, communicate with them, and meet their pressing personal needs.

The Savior's ministry was effective among those who had needs because of His inward sense of understanding human needs. He felt their sickness and suffering; their agony became His agony, and their burdens His burdens. Therefore when Christ ministered with a compassionate burden, he came into a oneness with His subjects. Out of the depth of this rapport, love abounded and the recipients were made completely whole.

The true Christian possesses the same unique compassionate qualities. This inherent quality is received after Christ is accepted through faith at the moment of repentance of every converted sinner. It is perfected when challenged by unjust actions of adversity and scorn.

Love has a hem to its garments
Which reaches the very dust;
It can touch the stains
Of the street and the lanes;
And because it can it must.
I ought to bend to the lowest,
I ought and therefore I can;
I was made to the end ,
That I might descend
In the steps of the Son of Man.

Author Unknown

Chapter Twelve

THE SUPREME SACRIFICE

"For God so loved the world that He gave His only begotten son." *(St. John 3:16)*

In the first chapter of this book we pointed out to you that when the first man, Adam, disobeyed the will of God by eating of the forbidden tree, sin came into existence upon the earth. Therefore, due to this rebellious action of the first man, a new urgent need was indeed born. Who could atone for man's sins? What could be done to rectify man's sinful action? Who or what could bring man back into fellowship and oneness with God?

Under the dispensation of Mosaic law various types of sacrifices and offerings were made for the atonement of man's universal corruption and shortcomings. But, all were insufficient to acquire salvation for mankind.

In spite of the miraculous deliverance of God's children out of the land of Egypt; in spite of all the great leaders such as Moses, Joshua and others whom God chose to lead his people, sin still raged in abundance with no mediator to bring man back into oneness with God.

Burnt offering and sacrifices became vain and displeasing in the presence of God. The blood of bullocks, lambs and goats were powerless to save.

God's attitude toward such sacrifices was conveyed explicitly through the Prophet Isaiah as he spoke the divine oracles of God in the following passage of scripture:

"Hear the word of the Lord, ye ruler of Sodom, give ear unto the law of our God, ye people of Gomorrah. To what purpose is the multitude of your sacrifices unto me? Sayeth the Lord, I am full of rams, and the fat of fed beast, and I delight not in the blood of bullocks, or of he goats. When ye come to appear before me, who hath required this at your hand to tread my courts? Bring no more vain oblations, incense is an abomination unto me, the new moons and Sabbaths, the calling of assemblies, I cannot away with, it is iniquity,

even the solemn meeting. Your new moons and your appointed feast my soul hateth, they are trouble unto me, I am weary to bear them. And when ye spread forth your hands, I will hide mine eyes from you, yea, when you make many prayers, I will not hear, your hands are full of blood. (Isaiah 1:10-15)

Man's greatest need was to have a Redeeming Savior who could genuinely atone for his sins. He needed someone who was akin to him in human likeness, and one who would be worthy in the sight of God for the challenging, agonizing task of rescuing mankind from his destined rendezvous with death and hell.

Through the prophet Isaiah the good news was proclaimed:

"For unto us a child is born unto us a son is given, and the government shall be upon his shoulder, and his name shall be called Wonderful, Counselor, The Mighty God, The Everlasting Father and The Prince of Peace.

Of the increase of his government and peace there shall be no end, upon the throne of David, and upon his kingdom, to order it, and to establish it with judgment and with justice from henceforth even forever. The zeal of the Lord of hosts will perform this." (Isaiah 9:6-7)

We see in the preceding prophetic discourse of Isaiah, the foretelling of the redeeming Savior's coming. We also see a revelation of the compound essence of his unique character. God sent Jesus in the likeness of sinful human flesh to die for man's sins, and to provide a miraculous means through which all men, both Jew and Gentile can receive a priceless inheritance – ETERNAL LIFE!

Not all the blood of beast
On Jewish altars slain
Could give the guilty conscience peace
Or wash away the stain.
But Christ, the heavenly Lamb,
Takes all our sins away.
A Sacrifice of nobler name,
And richer blood than they.

Isaac Watts

DR. EDDIE JERNAGIN

Chapter Thirteen

BORN AGAIN

A genuine *"born again"* experience rehabilitates the whole man. The most hardened criminal who yields his ways to Christ can be completely changed through the miracle of the *"Spiritual birth"* experience.

Society has now come into the awareness that severe physical punishment, imprisonment, reform programs, the gas chamber, the electric chair, and diverse forms of isolation do not really reform an individual. They are puzzled as to the reason for the non-effectiveness of such programs and processes.

The reason for such non-effectiveness is very simple, the problems of man are deeply rooted in the human spirit. Therefore, man's spirit nature is in need of reform. God has provided the means through which the *"sinful beast"* in man's nature can be changed through the spiritual process of reforming the whole soul of the man!

Only the Spirit of God working through Christ in man can balance, revive, restore, reform, and sanctify man wholly and, indeed, Holy!

Spiritual Ignorance Revealed

"There was a man of the Pharisees, named Nicodemus, a ruler of the Jews. The same came to Jesus by night, and said unto him, Rabbi, we know that thou art a teacher come from God, for no man can do these miracles that thou doest, except God be with him, Jesus answered and said unto him, Verily, verily I say unto thee, except a man be born again he cannot see the kingdom of God.

Nicodemus then asked Jesus the questions, How can a man be born when he is old? Can he enter the second time into his mother's womb, and be born?" (St. John3:1-4)

Even though Nicodemus was a religious man, and an astute intellectual scholar in Jewish law, the powerful truth of what Jesus was trying to convey to Nicodemus concerning the *"new birth"* was quite beyond his intellectual comprehension. He was academically competent but spiritually blind. The Jewish leader was totally ignorant of the spiritual implication of Christ's pronouncement.

There is a direct correlation between the spiritual blindness of Nicodemus and the spiritual blindness of many individuals today.

Too often, there are those who feel they have been *"born again"* because they shook the preacher's hand; or because their name is on the church roll; or perhaps, because they were baptized in water as a small child.

Sincere as these individuals may be, they are indeed, sincerely mistaken.

Awareness and Confession

A real *"Born again"* experience must involve a genuine awareness on the part of the person who seeks this experience that he or she is a sinner! This awareness first of all is expressed in honest confession.

"If we confess our sins he is faithful and just to forgive us our sin, and to cleanse us from all unrighteousness." (I John 1:9)

Repent

After genuine confession is made, repentance must then follow.

"Repent ye therefore and be converted, that you sins may be clotted out..." (Acts 3:9)

One must be willing to abandon and turn completely away from the things that are contrary to the will of God. The profile of the repentant person must go through a personal transition by immolating the personality of Christ.

Forsake

The third step to the *"new birth"* must involve positive action on behalf of one who seeks this experience to forsake and give up his sins. The Word of God tells us:

"Let the wicked forsake his way, and the unrighteous man his thoughts. And let him return unto the Lord, and he will have mercy upon him

and to our God, for he will abundantly pardon."
(Isa 55-7)

This step can be fortified each day of one's life by abiding in the whole truth of God's word. The more one lives and governs himself by God's word, the less sin will have dominion over him. The truth of God's word abiding within sets free from the bondage of sin.

"Ye shall know the truth and the truth shall set you free." (St. John 8:32)

When sin is forsaken by the repentant sinner, he no longer walks hand in hand with those things which can damn his soul. Instead, he takes on a new love which is Jesus Christ, in whom there is no sin. Thus, death, which is the inherent penalty for sin, no longer becomes his plight, but rather, he is destined for a new inheritance which is eternal life!

Believe

The fourth step to the *"new birth"* experience is of vital importance.

"He that cometh to God (the Bible declares), must believe that he is (that He is God, that he

exists) and that He is a rewarder of them that diligently seek him." *(Heb. 11:6)*

God has given to every man the capacity to believe and the Bible describes this as faith. One's faith must be released when seeking the *"regeneration experience."* Without believing that Christ died for your sins, all previous steps are nullified.

But, "If thou shalt confess with thy mouth the Lord Jesus, and shalt believe in thine heart that God hath raised him from the dead, thou shalt be saved." (Acts 16:31)

Receive

The final step to the complete transformation from death to life is that of joyously receiving Christ. If the exciting and exhilarating experience of the *"new birth"* is to become a reality in one's life, Christ must be received personally into the heart by faith. Extend to Christ your hospitality by receiving Him with thanks and praise, if you have not already done so!

"But as many as received Him, to them give He power to become the sons of God, even to them that believe on His name; Which were born, not of

blood, nor of the will of the flesh, nor of the will of man, but of God." (St. John 1:12-13)

How wonderful it is to possess and inherit the Kingdom of God within! It is a lifestyle based upon the righteousness of Christ Jesus.

He came to my desk with quivering lip –
The lesson was done.
"Dear Teacher I want a new leaf," he said.
"I have spoiled this one."
I took the old leaf, stained and blotted,
And gave him a new one, all unspotted,
And into his sad eyes, smiled,
"Do better now, my child!"
I went to the Throne with a quivering soul,
The old year was done.
"Dear Father, has thou a new leaf for me?
I have spoiled this one."
He took the old leaf, stained and blotted,
And gave me a new one, all unspotted,
And unto my sad heart smiled:
Do better now, my child!"

Author Unknown

Chapter Fourteen

FAITH

One of the most powerful gifts within the being of man is the measure of faith which he has inherited from God.

It is such a mysterious power that men do not understand the basic spiritual significance behind its function, they call it the "magic of the mind" or *"mind power."*

"He that cometh to God must believe that He is and that he is a rewarder of them that diligently seek him." (Hebrews 11:6)

There is no possible way anyone can have fellowship with the Lord God except through faith!

Faith, A Spiritual Power

For a man to have a meaningful relationship with his Creator he must possess a functional means through which he can communicate. God knowing this, implanted within the soul of human creation a spiritual power that brings man into spiritual togetherness with Him who is the Spirit.

"God is a Spirit, and they that worship him must worship Him in the spirit and in truth." (St. John 4:24)

The issuing of a measure of faith to every man is an expression of God's Divine concern for all of man's needs being fulfilled. It is a spiritual means provided by God through which the petitions of prayer can be relayed in the name of Jesus, thereby making spiritual communication possible for mankind to not only hear from heaven, but also to receive the miracles of heaven emitted from the hand of God.

Faith is a spiritual power influenced by belief, confidence and trust. It *"is the substance of things hopes for, the evidence of things not seen." (Hebrews 11:1)*

Just as a concrete foundation is the basis upon which a steadfast house stands; faith in Christ is the invisible spiritual basis upon which a spiritual house stands!

It is very important that every born again child of God and those who are aspiring to become one, know what faith will do. One's walk with God in

Christ is not a walk of *"physical sight"* but rather a walk of faith. From one's receiving the plan of salvation to the victorious rapture of the Saints, the entire successful venture of the Christian is inevitably determined by his faith and obedience to God.

Faith: A Seed

Have you ever pondered the fact that every form of matter you see around you started with a seed? It is a fact! Your favorite chair, the clothing you wear, the food you love to eat, even your own physical anatomy!

Faith can be compared to a seed. When a seed is planted in the ground and cultivated properly, in due time it springs forth as a tender, budding plant ready to yield forth a delicious fruit to be plucked during the golden harvest for the consumptive pleasure of man to fulfill his craving appetite.

When the seed of faith you have inherited is planted in the fertile words of God's promises for you, it will produce an abundant return. The fulfillment becomes your possession to meet your needs!

God's Word declares: *"if you have faith as a grain of mustard seed, you shall say unto the mountain, remove hence to yonder place , and it shall remove..." (Matt. 17:20)*

Monumental problems confronting mankind each day could easily be resolved if man would only release and plant his seed (faith) in God's Word. It is guaranteed to germinate! You reap what you sow!

Faith Works The Impossible

The Divine abilities of God can change impossibilities into tangible realities. Faith in Him is what makes the difference!

God does not always move within the context or realm of human possibilities. He is without a doubt a specialist in those things which many times are contrary to human reasoning and, also, the basic laws of nature.

Human reasoning, or common sense, says that when a man is dead there is no possible way he can live again. However, saving faith looks beyond the grip of death to a steadfast belief in Christ who says, *"he that believeth in me, though he were dead, yet shall he live." (St. John 11:35)*

This is inconceivable to human reasoning, but made possible through faith in Christ! The faith of Christ said, *"Take ye away the stone"* which sealed the grave of Lazarus, but the reasoning of Martha said, *"Lord, by this time he stinketh, for he hath been dead four days."*

The faith of Christ spoke again and demanded, "Lazarus, come forth." And in the final analysis faith produced that which was humanly impossible. Lazarus lived again! Supernatural faith always supersedes the so-called impossible.

Faith Used Daily

Whether you realize it or not, your faith is utilized in large measure every day. From the time you awake and take the unwinding morning stretch, until you retire for the night's siesta you unconsciously utilize a form of faith.

When you set the alarm clock, you have faith that the alarm will awaken you on time; when you put in a hard day's labor on your job, you have faith to believe that you will receive financial wages for your hours of labor; and when you recline to relax while flying in an airplane you have faith in the skills of the pilot, and the mechanics of the plane to get you to your destination safely. These, and many other daily occurrences in the life of individuals, activates a form of dependent trust characteristic of faith.

If in our everyday activities of life we choose to have faith in the physical properties constructed and designed by the hands of man, should we not have even more faith and confidence in the Great Infallible God who is Maker of us all? A God who is able to do, *"Exceeding, abundantly above all that we ask or think?" (Eph. 3:20)*

The wisdom and intellect which man used to develop aircraft, the automobile or the ships at sea can be attributed to the wisdom of God, who gave man the wisdom at the inception of creation. Therefore, why not have faith in the wisdom of God to help you with your pressing problems? Why not believe in Him to heal your sick body? Why not believe in Him to meet every particular need in your life?

All of this and more can be yours for the asking, your heritage of faith directed towards God makes it all possible!

Chapter Fifteen

HEALING

Gross sickness and disease linger in many parts of the world like a devouring curse feasting upon bodies and minds of countless thousands of human souls. Living bodies infected with malignant diseases lie in a state of helplessness yearning for just a few precious seconds of relief or the pampering touch of a comforting hand! Even though medical science has contributed remarkable various means to assist in the healing process, there are countless cases far beyond the ability of medical science to rectify.

The human body is God's creation. It is by far, second to none the most amazing matter ever created. Within the physical being of the human species, the Lord had built an inward biological healing system. For example, if you cut your finger and it requires stitching, it is not the stitching per se that heals the wound. It only aids the healing process that God has already implanted within the biological composition of the body. Medicine and drugs within themselves do not heal; they are used primarily for relieving and immunization measures. Unless the body's systems responds favorably to the medical treatment, the sickness or wound will persist.

The human organism before Adam's fall was not made to be the abode of sickness and disease. It is because of the imposing epidemic of sin that millions now suffer untold misery within their physical bodies! Even if you are a Christian, this does not exempt you from the possibility of ever encountering sickness or pain. Due to the abounding mercy of God, healing has become man's inherent gift. Within the Book of Books, the Bible, it is written: "I wish above all things that thou mayest prosper and be in health."

This particular excerpt of sacred utterance came from the Apostle John. It reveals sincere compassion and shows Christian character which reflects the sentiments of the desire of God for all his beloved children.

It stands to reason that any wise and conscientious inventor of a product should be able to diagnose malfunctions detected in his creation, and have means through which such abnormalities can be corrected. God who alone has made us all, has an unlimited scope of Supernatural power through which all sickness and disease must be subject.

"...with God all things are possible."

Therefore, terminal cases within themselves are only terminal in reference to man's inability to rectify. To those who choose to believe God for healing in spite of the failure of all human avenues, a miracle of healing is always within faith's reach!

Healing in a general sense is commonly denoted to imply the rectification of a physical abnormality such as a disease or sickness. Healing however, extends far beyond that of denoting it to a physical realm, Man has a contaminated spirit within his being that also requires healing and deliverance. The solution for spiritual cleansing has never, or ever shall be dependent upon medicine, scientific probing, or a scientific breakthrough discovered in a medical laboratory. There is only one sure proven solution for this type of healing and deliverance. That remedy is Jesus Christ!

Heaven is void of earth's plague characteristics, such as sickness and disease. Hence, healing which emanates in heaven is directed toward earth's inhabitants. It is transported through Divine Compassion, having its firm roots embedded within the treasured depths of the tender heart of Jesus Christ. It is by the stripes inflicted upon Him, because of our sins and sickness, that we can be healed and delivered from physical, mental and overall spiritual bondage.

Inheriting healing from Christ is what I envision as a divine healing transplant. By faith Christ's healing virtue is received into our sick bodies and minds thereby making the afflicted unequivocally whole!

Whenever Christ would touch those who were in need of healing, spiritual energy would flow from the Divine person of the Master into the physical being of His subjects.

"And when the men of that place had knowledge of him, they sent out into all that country round about, and brought unto him all that were diseased; and besought Him that they might only touch the hem of his garment; and as many as touched were made perfectly whole." (Matthew 14:35-36)

The event which occurred in the preceding text of scripture was manifested in reality countless times in the lives of those who sought the help of Christ during His earthly ministerial tenure. Those who desired His help and assistance for deliverance in their hour of spiritual, mental, and physical crises had but to take a simple step of faith by touching the hem of the Great Healer's garment to receive their deliverance.

"As many as touched..."

Received a new lease on life. They were healed!

Those who touched the Master Physician recognized He possessed a unique spiritual virtue of healing power which brought about instant results, and remedies for the needs in their lives. They genuinely confided in the fact that the very moment they touched Him the unbearable conditions of misery and frustration holding them captive would be dissolved instantly!

The woman who possessed an issue of blood for twelve years simply declared,

"...if I may but touch his clothes, I shall be whole." (Mark 5:28)

Therefore, when she took the initial step of faith and touched the hem of the Savior's garment, healing became her inheritance!

If in your hour of pain, suffering and mental bondage, you need a healing touch, reach out by faith to the Lord above,

"... and thine health shall spring forth speedily..." (Isaiah 58:8)

"And the whole multitude sought to touch him, for there went virtue out of him, and healed them all." (St. Luke 6:19)

Chapter Sixteen

TIME – YOUR HERITAGE

"To everything there is a season and a time to every purpose under heaven" (Ecc. 3:1)

All men have inherited "time." It is relative to human growth and development as well as a most valuable asset given man for attaining long and short range goals in life. It is a priceless commodity which gives man the chance to learn and apply his acquired knowledge into constructive accomplishments. Without it, history itself could not have been written because history requires a lapse of time before it can be classified as such. There would be no display of beautiful monuments, nor great halls of fame, had not the love of God bestowed *"time"* upon us all.

One's usage of this blessed heritage will determine not only what he will become today, but also what he will become in his eternal state of being, after the day of God's final judgment.

The Great Duel

Perhaps you can recall the amusing childhood story of the celebrated race between the hare and the turtle. The hare has acquired a proven reputation for his lightning swift speed. His hind legs were long and slender to precision. He was overwhelmingly confident he would win the duel and started off with swift physical zeal. But the obese turtle was not discouraged. He had short stubby legs and was extremely slow, but he utilized his time well. The cocky hare was so far ahead in the race that he stopped to take a refreshing siesta. He crossed his slender legs and fell asleep under a shade tree. While he was sleeping, time and the turtle passed him by. The consistent determined efforts of the clumsy turtle made him the champion. When the zealous hare awakened out of his sleep, much to his amazing surprise and embarrassing disappointment, time had expired. The proud turtle was already on the victory stand.

There are countless millions who have awakened to the awareness of what they could have been in life, but due to yielding to the *"snaring vice"* of procrastination, time has swiftly passed them by.

It is too late now to become what they could have been.

The Issued Talents

Consider the parable of the issued talents we read of in the Gospel of St. Matthew 25:13-14. Each servant was given talents; to one was issued five, to another two and to another one. The superior gave to each servant according to his ability to perform the job assigned. Each servant had time to utilize his own individual abilities. However, after the allotted time had expired for the assignment, two of the servants had performed commendably and brought back an increase. But the workman who had been given one talent did not value his assignment nor his given time to perform the duty. Therefore he came back to his superior empty handed and full of excuses.

Each servant was given a just recompense of reward. The slothful servant was rebuked and lost his soul!

The day of judgment shall be in a similitude of this parable. Only you and I will be servants, and God shall be the Judge. What will he say to us? What will our reward be? Will we have used our inherited time well, or will we have an excuse?

There are too many who spend all their God-given time working for themselves! There are too many who sit idly and *"watch the rest of the world go by"* without contributing anything constructive for its betterment. There are too many who spend their time complaining and finding fault, but never setting a good example themselves for others to follow! While such faults and failures linger, *"time"* still marches on!

The human race has before it the example of the Creator who utilized time to its fullest. In the Divine Mind of God there was devised a plan to change the massive void which existed prior to the creation of life.

God, therefore plunged into the task of turning His vision into reality. You and I have but to look around us and see that He did His job superbly well. God had set the time of six says to do His work. He valued the time in which He had assessed Himself to perform the miracle of creation.

"And God saw everything that he had made, and, behold, it was very good. And the evening and the morning were the sixth day." *(Genesis 1:31)*

"Thus the heavens and the earth were finished, and all the host of them. And on the seventh day,

God ended his work which he had made; and he rested on the seventh day form all his work which he had made." (Genesis 2:1-2)

If you live to be seventy years old, and you are now thirty, time is in your favor! But, if you have reached your senior years, time is certainly not as long as it has been for you. Nevertheless, no man, young or old, has a monopoly on time. Therefore, one should live as though each day were his last, and value the time thereof!

Time is not prejudiced as to position, nor is it swayed by the color of a man's skin. It is not disrespectful. Time does not show favoritism. It has a job to perform, and it is always on schedule even to the smallest fraction!

What a travesty it is to waste such a valuable gift as *"time"*. It is a precious asset we are given by God to dream of positive events and watch our dreams become reality!

It is by this wonderful gift that we have precious moments to enjoy those we love, and reach the height of our positive potential.

It is through this invaluable gift of "time" that we can explore the vast expanse of life and fulfill the joy of life's purpose. Why not use the wondrous gift of *"time"* wisely; and when your earthly tenure is ended let the legacy of your time testify to those who remain and are yet to come about the importance of using their inheritance of *"time"* pursuing noble goals!

MAN'S INHERITANCE

Time is money –

We have no right to waste it.

Time is power –

We have no right to dissipate it.

Time is influence –

We have no right to throw it away.

Time is life –

We must value it greatly.

Time is God's

He gives it to us for a purpose.

Time is a sacred trust –

We must answer for every moment.

Time is wisdom –

We have no right to be ignorant.

Time is preparation for eternity

We must redeem it.

Author Unknown

Chapter Seventeen

OMEGA

When traveling down a highway, the closer you get to a town or city, the more advertising signs you see telling one what to expect as he reaches the city and also how to get there.

Life is like traveling down a highway toward a specific destination. The closer man nears his eternal state of being, the more prophetic signs begin unfolding, revealing the true essence of the predictions made by the prophets of old.

As the activities of this present life enters its climactical extremity, one can see along the highway of life, literal prophetic fulfillment of *"wars and rumors of wars"*, *"earthquakes in diverse places"* the barren desert place of Israel blossoming like a rose, Israel becoming an independent nation and Jews by the thousands returning to their beloved homeland, the *"pouring out of God's Spirit upon all flesh,"* the cry of peace, but sudden destruction, etc., not withstanding, even though these and countless other signs exist, testifying to the end of time, they yet go unheeded by the majority.

Time is a relative reality in the lives of all. How one spends his time traveling through life will greatly influence his eternity.

Consequently, since man is a flesh being and subjected to human fallacy, God's *"truth"* exists to inform man as he travels the highway of this life, that he must merge his life and ways submissively into the hands of Christ who is everlastingly secure.

When coming to the end of a dual or multi-lane highway, if you are driving in a lane which will eventually run out, a posted sign will inform you of such.

You will eventually have to merge with the lane that continues, or suffer the consequences of a severe accident, placing your life in jeopardy. Common sense tells you to obey the signs and follow instructions!

Life consists of two figurative highways. Each leads to an eternal destiny. For the purpose of simplification, we shall name them Highway *"L"* and highway *"D"*. It is your privilege to travel the highway of your choice.

For just a few moments let's you and I take a visionary tour of each highway.

Highway D – Journey to Hell

Highway *"D"* is the broad bustling thoroughfare to hell. It is often referred to as the *"downward road"*. Along its route travels: 1) the *"hip generation"*, 2) the sinner, 3) the atheist, 4) the agnostic, 5) the *"sun worshiper"*, 6) the racist, 7) the murderer, 8) the thief, 9) the backsliding Christian, 10) the crooked politician, 11) the crooked clergy, 12) the liar, 13) the gambler, 14) the transgressor, 15) the hypocrite, etc. I could go on but this volume could not contain the unlimited factions! God himself is the Supreme Judge, therefore only He knows!

If you are a Christian and believe there is no pleasure traveling the *"downward road"*, I would like to disillusion you. There are pleasures galore! In fact, the route to hell is so exciting that multiplied millions are charmed into its mainstream to partake of the camouflaged venom.

The momentary pleasure and excitement encountered while on the *"downward road"* ultimately leads to death! This is the inheritance of those who choose to journey contrary to God's Divine Master Plan for earthly living.

The Devil

The chief architect of the road to hell is Lucifer, better known to many by the title of *"Satan"* or the *"devil"*. And contrary to one's childhood belief, he does not have a long tail, nor is he red in color. By all means, he does not carry a pitchfork!

To the contrary, prior to his fall from heaven, he was an angel of light likened unto the glowing planet Venus. *"When appearing as the morning star."* But now, he moves in his demonic state as a *"spirit"* of darkness, infecting the human mind with the deadly disease of sin.

Hades

At the end of Highway *"D"* there exists eternal torment for rebellious souls in the bottomless abode of hades. Ungodly men weeping uncontrollably, cry for relief, but there is none. The rich who in the pinnacle of prosperity looked down upon the poor and refused to give even a crumb, now plead with God to send the poor, that they may dip the tips of their fingers in water, to cool their parched tongues. But the great gulf which separates the eternally lost from those who are now the eternal "sons of God" make it virtually impossible.

A Plea From Hell

From the deep crevices of hell another plea is heard:

"I pray therefore, father that thou wouldst send him to my father's house; For I have five brethren, that he may testify unto them, lest they also come into this place of torment.

Abraham sayeth unto him, they have Moses and the prophets, let them hear them.

And he said, Nay, father Abraham, but if one went unto them form the dead, they will repent.

And he said unto him, if they hear not Moses and the prophets, neither will they be persuaded, though one rose from the dead." (St. Luke 16:27-31)

Wrath and Hell

There are those who choose to believe that hell and torment in the literal sense is nothing more than a *"way out"* fantasy in the minds of fundamentalist believers. The non-fundamentalist envision God to be a God of mild attributes, full of mercy, love and compassion. This is very true. Nevertheless, God is also a God of wrath which can be vividly detected in the prophetic discourse of Isaiah:

"Behold, the day of the Lord cometh, cruel both with wrath and fierce anger, to lay the land desolate, and he shall destroy the sinners thereof out of it.

For the stars of heaven and the constellations thereof shall not give their light, the sun shall be darkened in his going forth, and the moon shall not cause her light to shine.

And I will punish the world for their evil, and the wicked for their iniquity, and I will cause the arrogance of the proud to cease, and will lay low the haughtiness of the terrible." (Isa.13:9-11)

For those who oppose the thought of wrath and hell it may bring consolation to know that hell and wrath is not the inheritance of God's obedient children. God cares intimately for mankind. However, hell and wrath is the inheritance of the devil and his angels. If in man's freedom of choice he chooses to become an advocate or servant of sin and avaricious greed, he in turn makes hell his free choice and inevitable eternal inheritance. The *"downward road"* takes you there.

Highway "L:" – Journey to New Jerusalem

As our next journey begins, we are now traveling along highway *"L"*. This is the route to "eternal life." It is a straight and narrow thoroughfare immensely busy at this stage of our adventure. Everyone seems to be excited about the thought of reaching the incomparable paradise called the *"New Jerusalem."*

For millenniums, generations have traveled this same route with a craving passion to inhabit this vast heavenly city not made with hands.

Moving briskly along our adventurous tour, we notice the posted signs along the way which have unique inscriptions written on them, such as:

"... he that endureth to the end shall be saved." (Matt. 10:22)

"...behold I make all things new..." (Rev. 21:5)

"... straight is the gate, and narrow is the way, which leadeth unto life, and few there be that find it." (Matt. 7:14)

I could not help but intensely focus on the last signboard which we just passed. Its inscription is a perfect correlation of our immediate surroundings at this point of our odyssey.

I clearly recall when we started on our excursion that there were many who started with us, but for some strange reason as we get nearer our destination, the number of travelers is getting smaller, and many are detouring.

"Oh how narrow is the door, and how difficult is the road which carries to life, and few are those who are found on it." (The New Testament according to the Eastern Text)

Our epic journey has been long and trying. Through many pitfalls we have come; humiliation, we've experienced. Tears of agony we have shed. We've come too far to turn around.

Our faith has brought us victoriously thus far, and there shall be no turning back. The clouds of gloom have encamped round about us, but do or die, our unshakable faith tells us "we shall overcome!"

At Last

BEHOLD! Coming down just beyond the horizon. Such radiance and luminous splendor mortal eyes have never beheld! Could this be our destined goal? Could this really be the "New Jerusalem" coming down out of heaven? Oh! Would he who is so Preciously Divine condescend to mortal earthly creatures such as we? As you and I gaze in awe at such majestic beauty our voices are stilled. And then all of a sudden, like a mighty roaring thunder, he who is angelic begins to speak:

"Behold the tabernacle of God is with men, and he will dwell with them, and they shall be his people, and God himself shall be with them, and be their God!" (Rev. 21:3)

"And he that sat upon the throne said, Behold I make all things new!" (Rev 21:5)

City of Jeweled Foundations

Such a beautiful city, the New Jerusalem! Its brilliant light is likened unto a radiant jasper stone, transparent as a crystal. The light is the glory of God. Therefore, there is no need for the sun or moon to shine. Christ, the lamb of God shall eternally light our way!

The walls of this reigning city are made of jasper. It is, in fact, a city of pure gold. The firm foundations of the great wall which surrounds her are constructed of the finest stones.

"The first foundation made of jasper; the second, sapphire, the third, chalcedony; the fourth, an emerald; the fifth, sardonyx; the sixth, sardius; the seventh, chrysolite; the eighth, beryl; the ninth, a topaz; the tenth, a chrysoprasus; the eleventh; a jacinth and the twelfth, an amethyst." (Rev. 21:19)

Incomparable Paradise

The heavenly city is truly an incomparable paradise! Within her glory there exists a "spiritual temple." Which makes it possible to eliminate formal traditional worship within the enclosure of man made walls. The Lord God Omnipotent and the Lamb are the temple thereof. So invincible is the strength of this mighty fortress, it cannot be destroyed by nuclear warfare. Neither will it ever be decayed by the toll of time.

Within this New Jerusalem the being of man is immortal. Immortality is his bestowed inheritance.

Therefore, he can sing continuously and praise the Lamb of God forever without being exhausted.

The agony of physical pain is no longer a thorn in the flesh for the immortal soul. Spiritual immunization from sickness, disease, mental pressure, death and fear is the "overcomer's" inheritance!

The *"river of life"* flows freely in the New Jerusalem, spewing forth out of the throne of God, shading its celestial shore, there stands the *"tree of life,"* consisting of sweet smelling leaves with healing properties for the nations!

"Blessed are they that do his commandments that they may have right to the tree of life, and may enter in through the gates into the city!" (Rev 22:14)

WHERE WILL YOU SPEND YOUR INHERITED ETERNITY?

OMEGA

Ah! Who upon earth can conceive
The bliss that with Jesus we'll share?
Or who this dark world would not leave,
And earnestly long to be there?
There Christ is the light and the sun,
His glories unhinderedly shine;
Already our joy is begun,
our rest is the glory divine.
'Tis good, at His word, to be here,
Yet better, e'en now to be gone;
And there in His presence appear,
And rest where He rests on the throne.
Yet Ah! What great joy 'twill afford,
When Him we shall see in the air;
And enter the joy of the Lord,
Forever to be with Him there.

Charles Wesley

ABOUT THE AUTHOR

At the age of eighteen, Eddie Jernagin accepted the Divine Call to minister and over the many years his powerful and practical words have been a blessing to countless thousands!

For 37 years, Dr. Eddie Jernagin pastured the Christ Is The Answer Church in Los Angeles, California. He is a noted Conference Speaker, Counselor, Bible Teacher, Adviser, International Radio Personality, Author and Bishop.

In 2012, he founded and is the president of **"New Dimensions International Ministries."** It's the evangelistic Bible Preaching and Teaching Ministry of Dr. Jernagin that's taking the Gospel of Jesus Christ unto the whole world.

Dr. Eddie Jernagin is a gifted writer of practical truth endeavoring to share vivid insights about life from a biblical perspective. He aspires to show how utilizing biblical principles as a guideline can provide righteous solutions for human kind to ultimately succeed beyond all negative obstacles.

Dr. Eddie Jernagin also serves as the Vice Prelate of the Governing Board and the Bishop of the Fourth Jurisdiction of The Convention Of Covenanting Churches.

His messages will inspire you to search the scriptures, study the Kingdom Principles of God, mature in your faith, listen and obey The Holy Spirit and walk in the victorious life that Christ has given you.

MORE AVAILABLE BOOKS BY BISHOP EDDIE JERNAGIN

Man's Inheritance

Fulfilling Your Purpose

Communicating With God

Faith Building Exhortations

Opening The Door To A New Millennium

Wise Advice and Revelation Insights

The Blessing of Tough Experiences

Devising A Christian Marketing Strategy

MINISTRY CONTACT INFORMATION

Dr. Eddie Jernagin

New Dimension International Ministries

PO Box 976

MUNCIE, IN 47308

Website:

www.eddiejernagin.com

Email:

bishopeddiej@aol.com

www.ingramcontent.com/pod-product-compliance
Lightning Source LLC
LaVergne TN
LVHW051125080426
835510LV00018B/2237